W9-BXT-426

FREDERICK COUNTY PUBLIC LIBRARIES

NORTH AMERICAN ANIMALS
Coyotes

by Chris Bowman

BLASTOFF! READERS
3

BELLWETHER MEDIA • MINNEAPOLIS, MN

Note to Librarians, Teachers, and Parents:

Blastoff! Readers are carefully developed by literacy experts and combine standards-based content with developmentally appropriate text.

Level 1 provides the most support through repetition of high-frequency words, light text, predictable sentence patterns, and strong visual support.

Level 2 offers early readers a bit more challenge through varied simple sentences, increased text load, and less repetition of high-frequency words.

Level 3 advances early-fluent readers toward fluency through increased text and concept load, less reliance on visuals, longer sentences, and more literary language.

Level 4 builds reading stamina by providing more text per page, increased use of punctuation, greater variation in sentence patterns, and increasingly challenging vocabulary.

Level 5 encourages children to move from "learning to read" to "reading to learn" by providing even more text, varied writing styles, and less familiar topics.

Whichever book is right for your reader, Blastoff! Readers are the perfect books to build confidence and encourage a love of reading that will last a lifetime!

This edition first published in 2016 by Bellwether Media, Inc.

No part of this publication may be reproduced in whole or in part without written permission of the publisher. For information regarding permission, write to Bellwether Media, Inc., Attention: Permissions Department, 5357 Penn Avenue South, Minneapolis, MN 55419.

Library of Congress Cataloging-in-Publication Data

Bowman, Chris, 1990- author.
  Coyotes / by Chris Bowman.
     pages cm. – (Blastoff! Readers. North American Animals)
  Summary: "Simple text and full-color photography introduce beginning readers to coyotes. Developed by literacy experts for students in kindergarten through third grade"– Provided by publisher.
  Audience: Ages 5-8
  Audience: K to grade 3
  Includes bibliographical references and index.
  ISBN 978-1-62617-259-3 (hardcover: alk. paper)
  1. Coyote–Juvenile literature. I. Title.
  QL737.C22B67 2016
  599.77'25–dc23
                                                          2014050316

Text copyright © 2016 by Bellwether Media, Inc. BLASTOFF! READERS and associated logos are trademarks and/or registered trademarks of Bellwether Media, Inc. SCHOLASTIC, CHILDREN'S PRESS, and associated logos are trademarks and/or registered trademarks of Scholastic Inc.

Printed in the United States of America, North Mankato, MN.

Table of Contents

What Are Coyotes?

Coyotes are common **mammals** in North America.

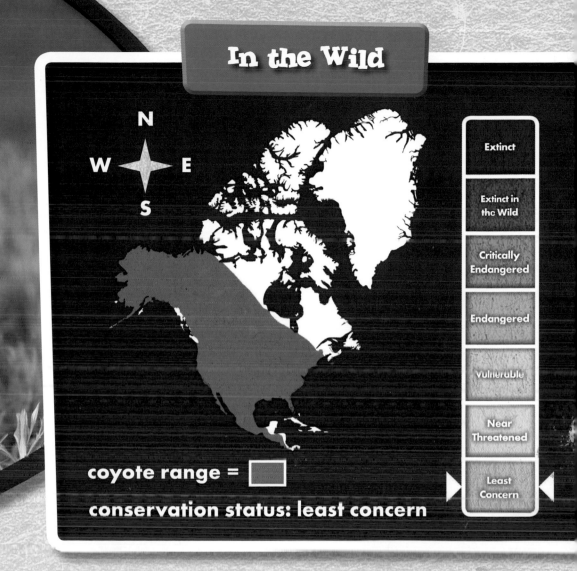

In the Wild

N W E S

coyote range = ☐

conservation status: least concern

Extinct

Extinct in the Wild

Critically Endangered

Endangered

Vulnerable

Near Threatened

Least Concern

These animals live all over the **continent**. They are found from northern Canada to Panama.

They **adapt** to many **habitats**.
They can be spotted in prairies
and deserts.

Others live in mountains and forests. Some coyotes even live in cities.

Identify a Coyote

bushy tail **long ears** **narrow face**

Many different colors make up a coyote's coat. Their fur is usually a mix of gray, red, brown, and black. White fur covers their bellies.

They have bushy tails with either a white or black tip.

They weigh up to 50 pounds (23 kilograms). Their bodies are up to 37 inches (94 centimeters) long. Their tails grow to about 16 inches (41 centimeters) long.

eastern coyote

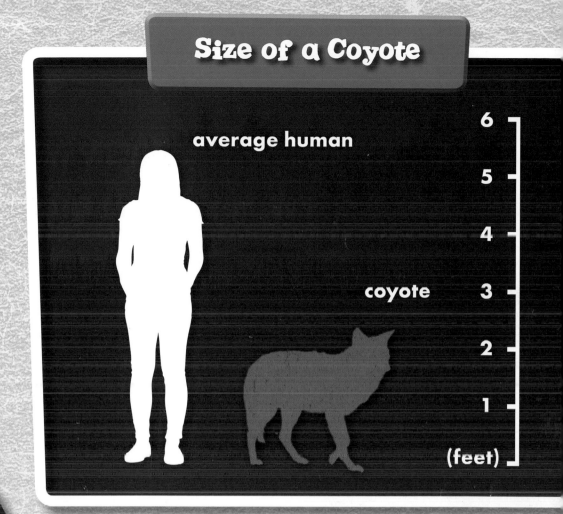

Size of a Coyote

average human

coyote

6
5
4
3
2
1
(feet)

Coyotes may be different sizes depending on where they live. Eastern coyotes are the biggest.

In Their Territory

Coyotes often live alone or in pairs. They guard a **territory** where they live and hunt.

Their **den** is the center of this area.
Coyotes dig their dens in the ground
using their paws. Dens can also be
under rocks, trees, or bushes.

They often hunt small animals throughout their territory. Coyotes chase rabbits, **rodents**, birds, and insects.

On the Menu

white-tailed deer

deer mice

cottontail rabbits

snowshoe hares

gray squirrels

prickly pear cactuses

Sometimes no **prey** is available. Then these **omnivores** search for fruits, vegetables, and **carrion**.

With the Pack

In winter, coyotes form **packs** to hunt. The pack is led by a **dominant** pair.

The coyotes work together to take down larger animals like moose or deer. They can run up to 40 miles (64 kilometers) per hour to catch their prey.

Raising Pups

In spring, females give birth to **pups**. They stay in the den to **nurse**. After about three weeks, the pups leave the den to play.

Name for babies:	pups
Size of litter:	3 to 12 pups
Length of pregnancy:	2 months
Time spent with parents:	9 months

Parents feed their pups until they are about 9 months old. In packs, older siblings may help raise the pups.

Then the young coyotes can start a pack of their own!

Glossary

adapt—to become comfortable with something

carrion—the rotting meat of a dead animal

continent—one of the seven land areas on Earth

den—a sheltered place; coyotes dig dens underground, under rocks, or in hollow trees.

dominant—commanding or leading

habitats—lands with certain types of plants, animals, and weather

mammals—warm-blooded animals that have backbones and feed their young milk

nurse—to drink mom's milk

omnivores—animals that eat both plants and animals

packs—groups of coyotes that live and hunt together

prey—animals that are hunted by other animals for food

pups—baby coyotes

rodents—small animals that gnaw on their food

territory—the land area where an animal lives

To Learn More

AT THE LIBRARY

Leaf, Christina. *Gray Wolves*. Minneapolis, Minn.: Bellwether Media, 2015.

Roza, Greg. *Your Neighbor the Coyote*. New York, N.Y.: Windmill Books, 2012.

Spilsbury, Louise. *Coyote*. Chicago, Ill.: Heinemann Library, 2011.

ON THE WEB

Learning more about coyotes is as easy as 1, 2, 3.

1. Go to www.factsurfer.com.

2. Enter "coyotes" into the search box.

3. Click the "Surf" button and you will see a list of related web sites.

With factsurfer.com, finding more information is just a click away.

Index

The images in this book are reproduced through the courtesy of: Mircea Costina, front cover, pp. 16-17; Tier und Naturfotografie/ Superstock, pp. 4-5; J & C Sohns/ Tier und Naturfotografie/ Superstock, pp. 6-7; Bobby Deal, p. 7; Jeannette Kutzir Photog, p. 8 (top left); karl umbriaco, p. 8 (top middle); Matt Knoth, p. 8 (top right); gabriel12, p. 8 (bottom); ArmanWerthPhotography, p. 9; Kitchin and Hurst/ Glow Images, pp. 10-11; Tom Walker/ Corbis, p. 12; Geoffrey Kuchera, pp. 12-13; Critterbiz, pp. 14-15; James Pierce, p. 15 (top left); Close Encounters Photo, p. 15 (top right); Michael Chatt, p. 15 (middle left); Tom Reichner, p. 15 (middle right); Michael Rowlandson, p. 15 (bottom left); Scisetti Alfio, p. 15 (bottom right); Gerard Lacz Images/ Superstock, p. 17; Holly Kuchera, pp. 18-19; Lynn Bystrom, p. 19; Debbie Steinhausser, p. 20; Juniors Bildarchiv/ Glow Images, p. 21.